MATTEO

CARCASSI

T0210280

Op.60

For Guitar

Edited and Performed
By Paul Henry

To access audio visit:
www.halleonard.com/mylibrary

Enter Code
4018-5276-1160-4482

ISBN 978-0-7935-1867-8

HAL•LEONARD®

7777 W. BLUEMOUND RD. P.O. BOX 13819 MILWAUKEE, WI 53213

Visit Hal Leonard Online at
www.halleonard.com

MATTEO

CARCASSI

(1792-1853)

ike any instrument, the guitar has adopted certain collections of etudes that are considered essential for the serious student. Matteo Carcassi's *25 Melodic and Progressive Studies, Op. 60*, along with the works of Sor, Giuliani, Tarrega, Aguado, Villa-Lobos and others, is such a collection, and offers wonderful insights into the musical and technical ideas of one of the guitar's most prominent figures. With a careful approach to the study of these works, the guitarist will discover many important aspects of right and left hand technique which remain as relevant today as they were in Carcassi's time. Equally important, the musical ideas make each piece an attractive performance vehicle.

Carcassi composed these studies in a rather straightforward fashion; the musical and technical concepts are readily apparent, allowing the guitarist to perform them with equal attention to clarity of articulation, tone, dynamics, and melodic line.

Paul Henry

CONTENTS

No. 1

Matteo Carcassi

No. 2

Moderato con espressivo

No. 3

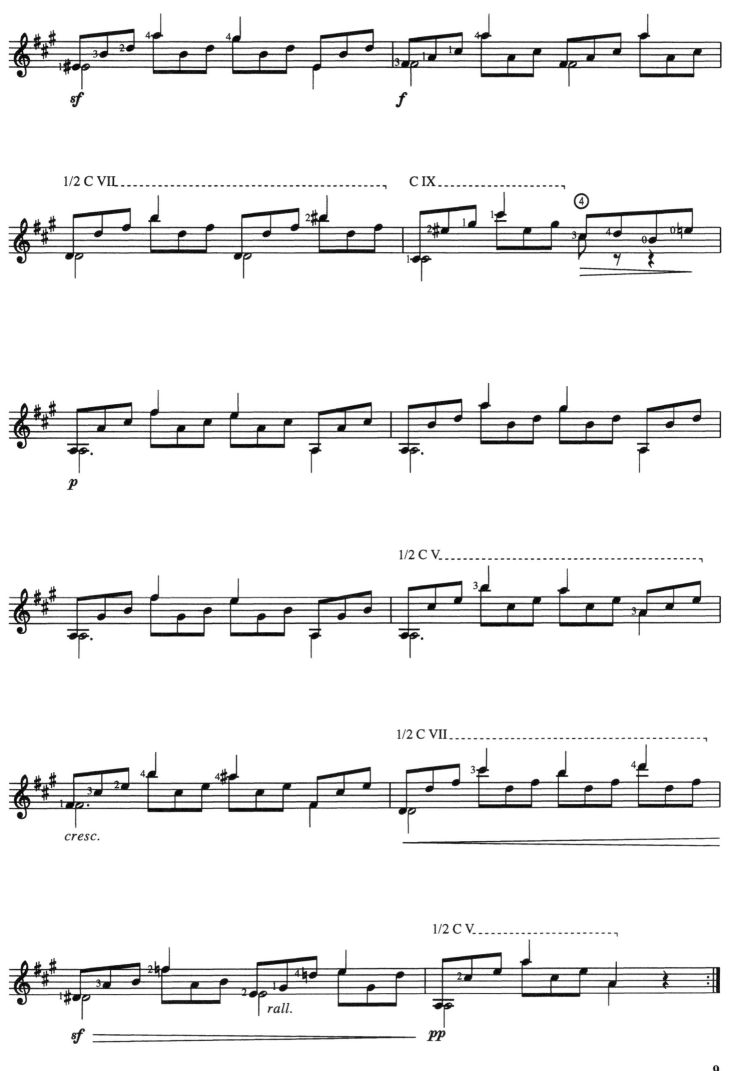

No. 4

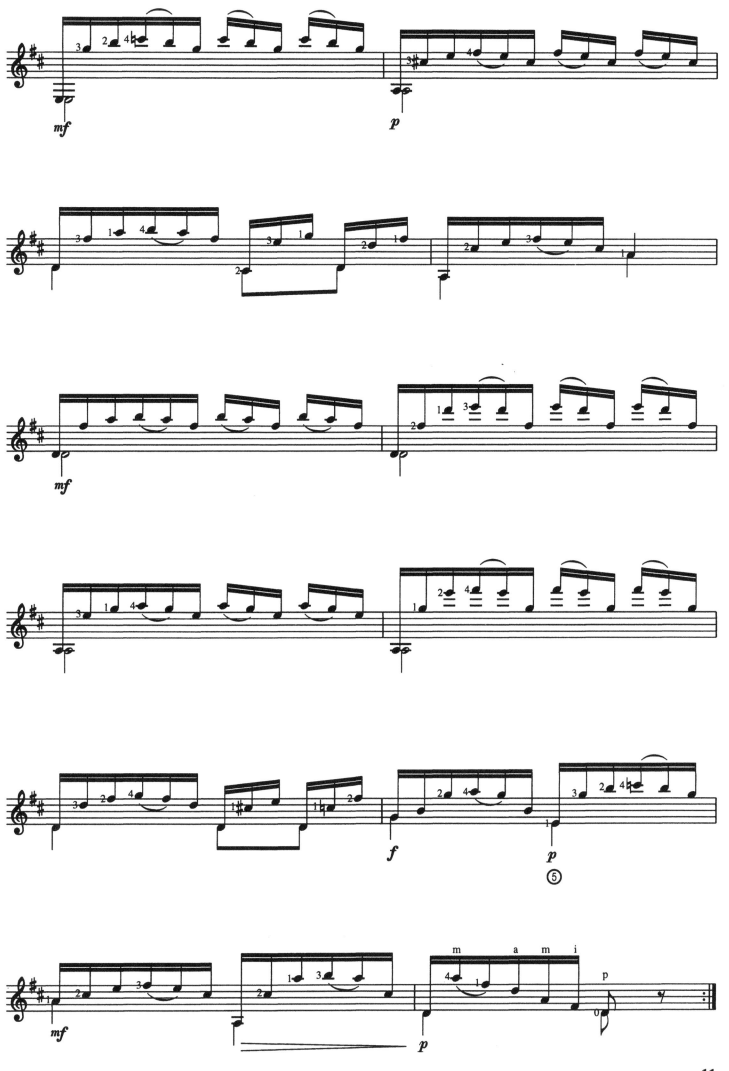

No. 5

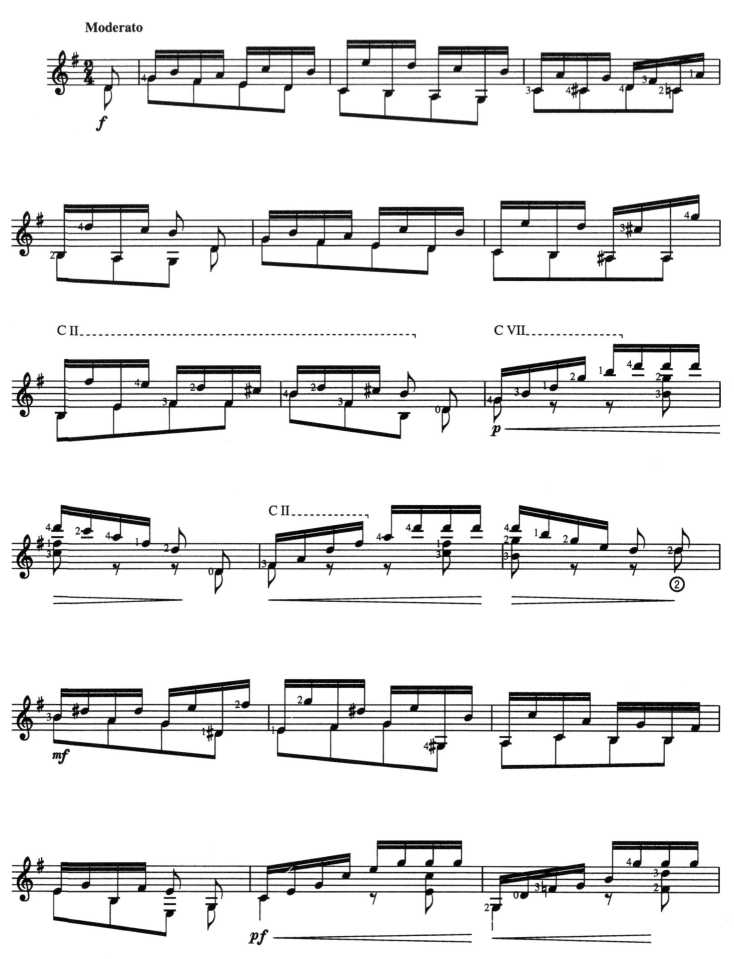

No. 6

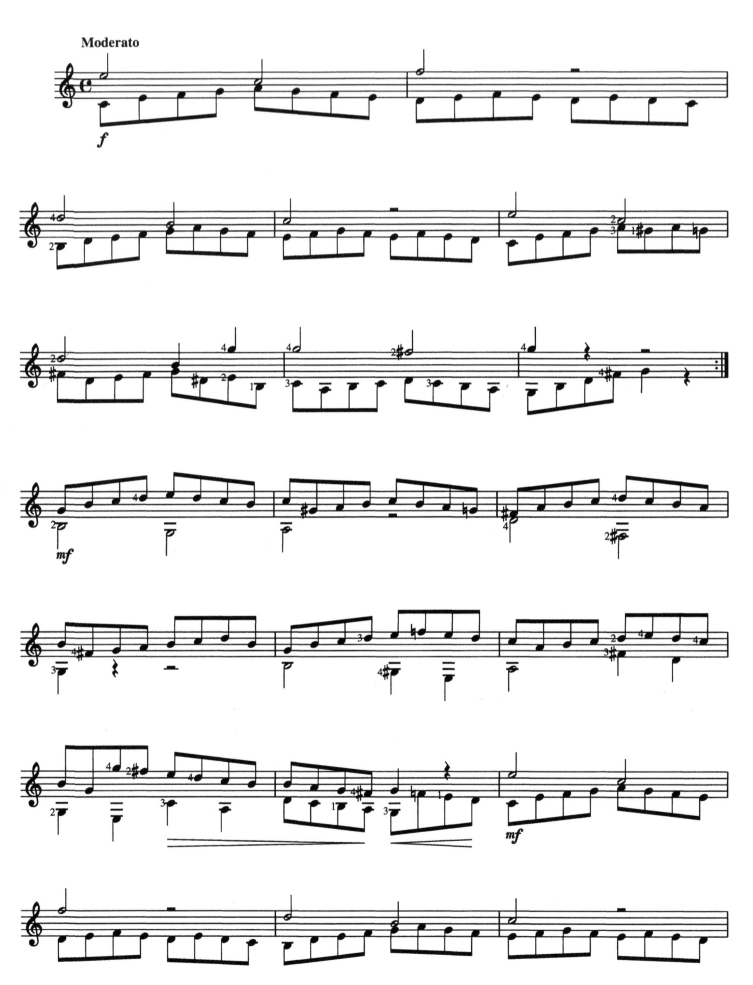

No. 7

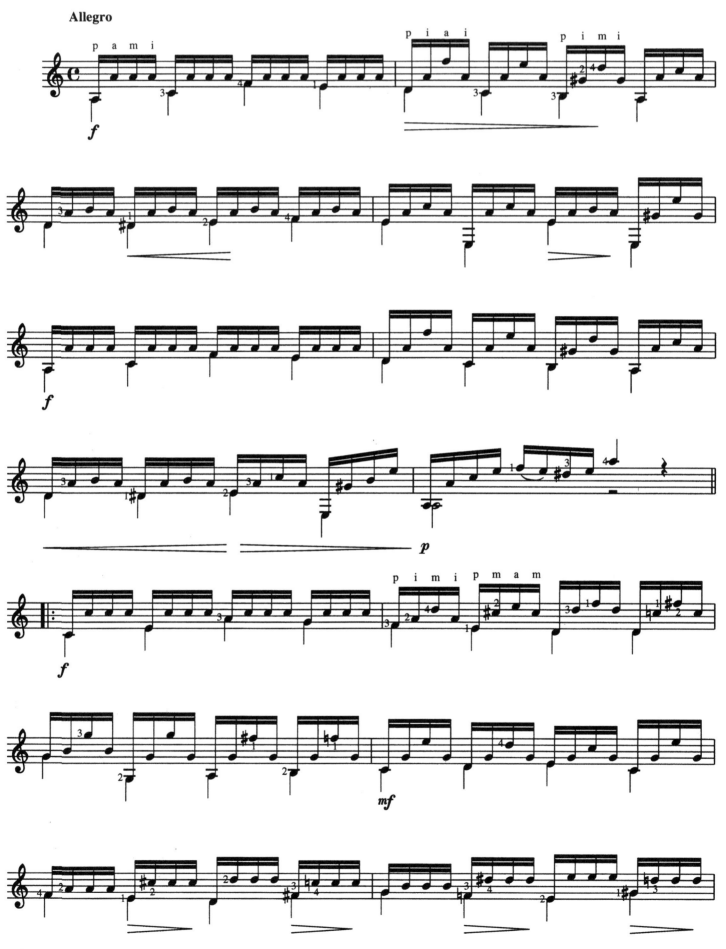

No. 8

No. 9

No. 10

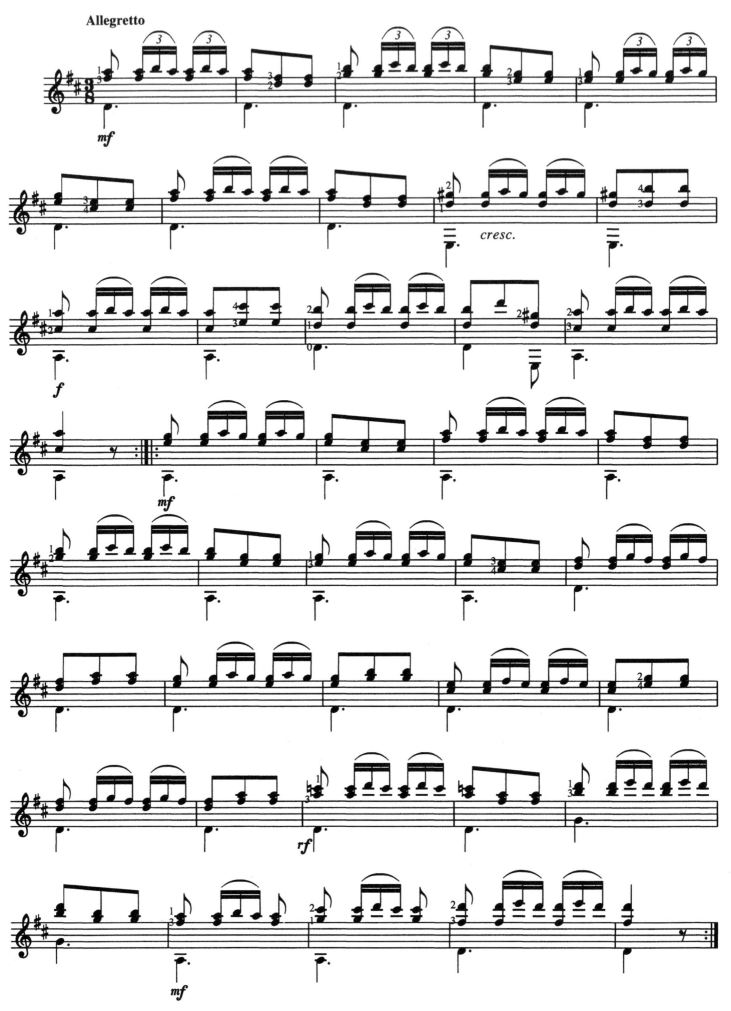

No. 11

No. 12

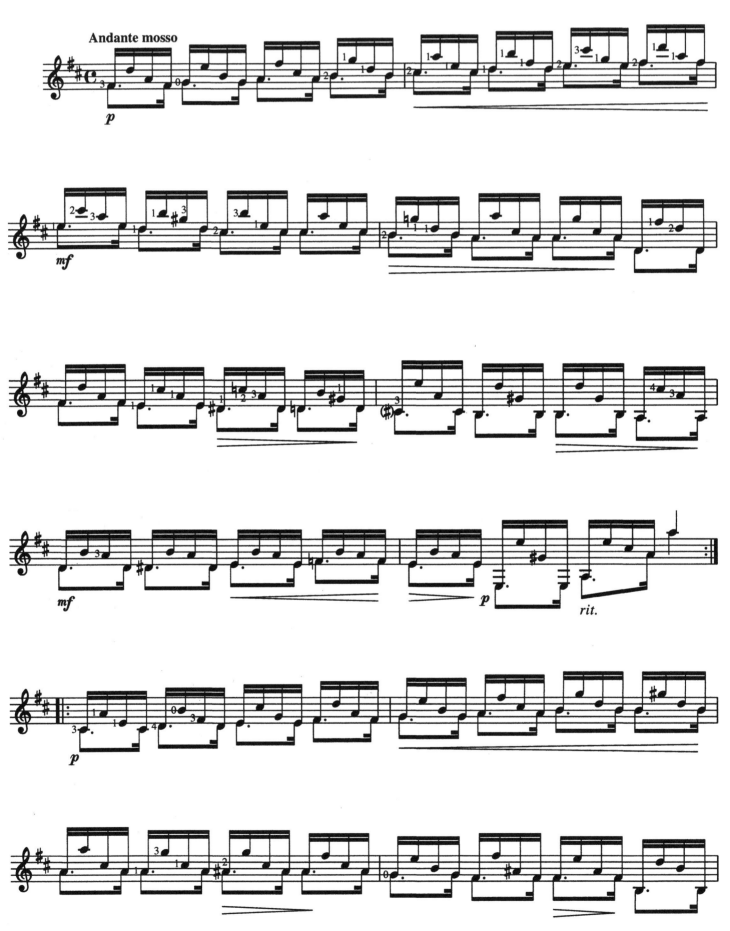

No. 13

Andantino grazioso

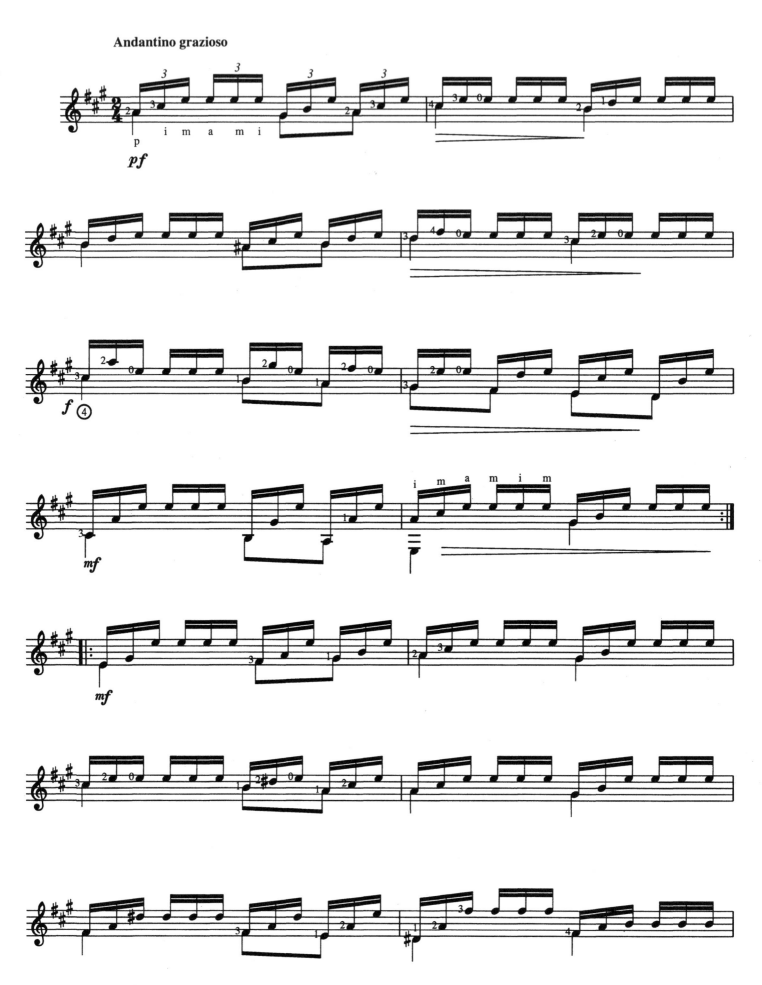

25

No. 14

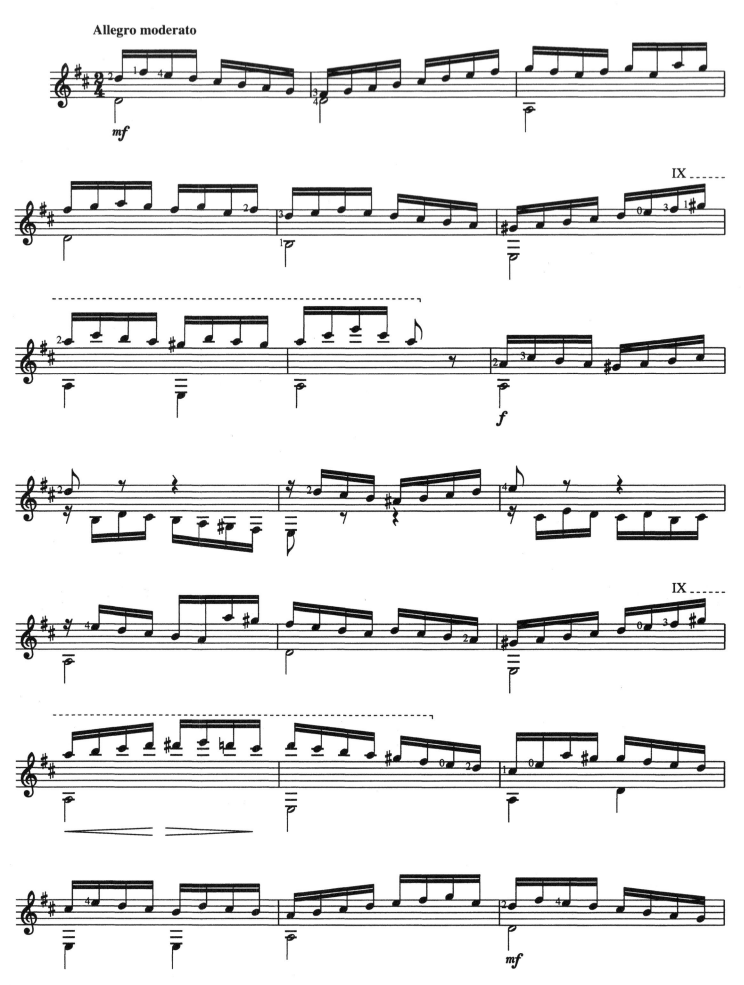

No. 15

No. 16

No. 17

Moderato

No. 18

No. 19

Allegro moderato

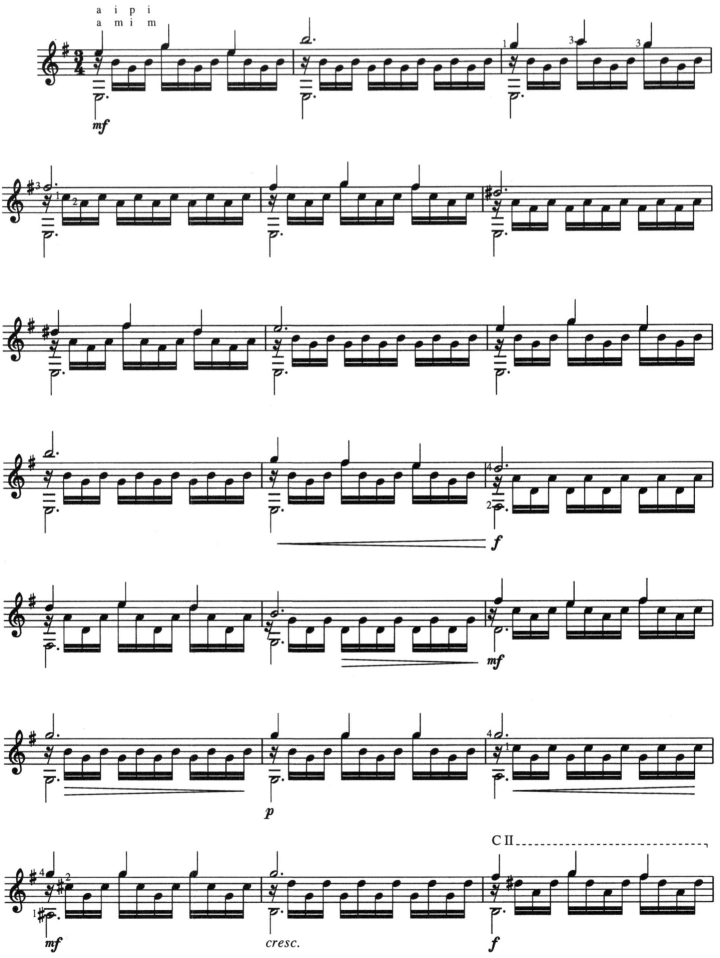

No. 20

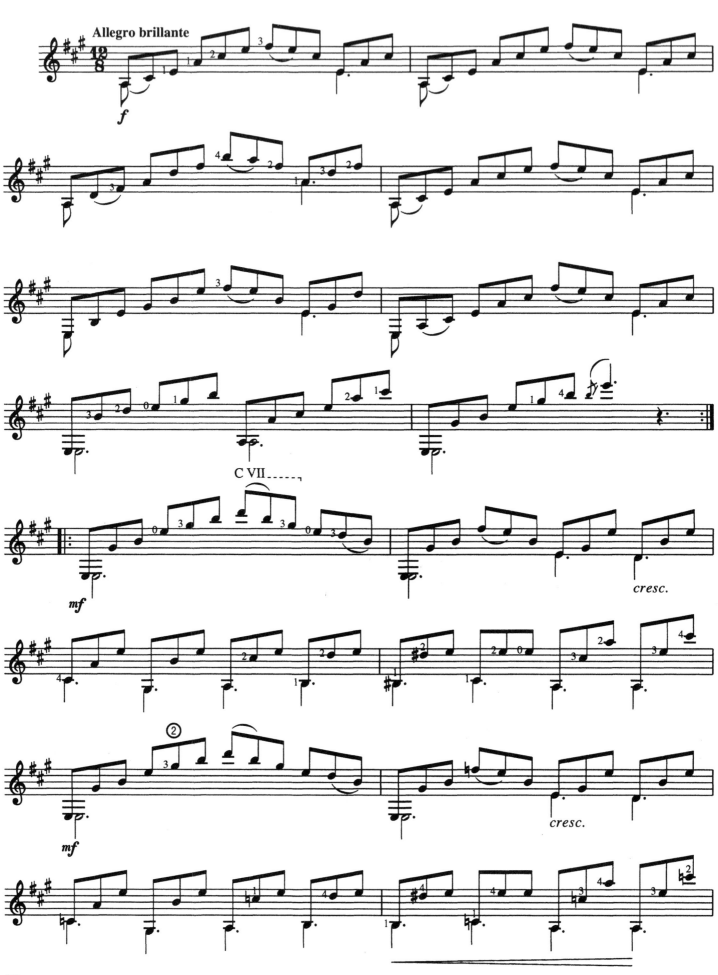

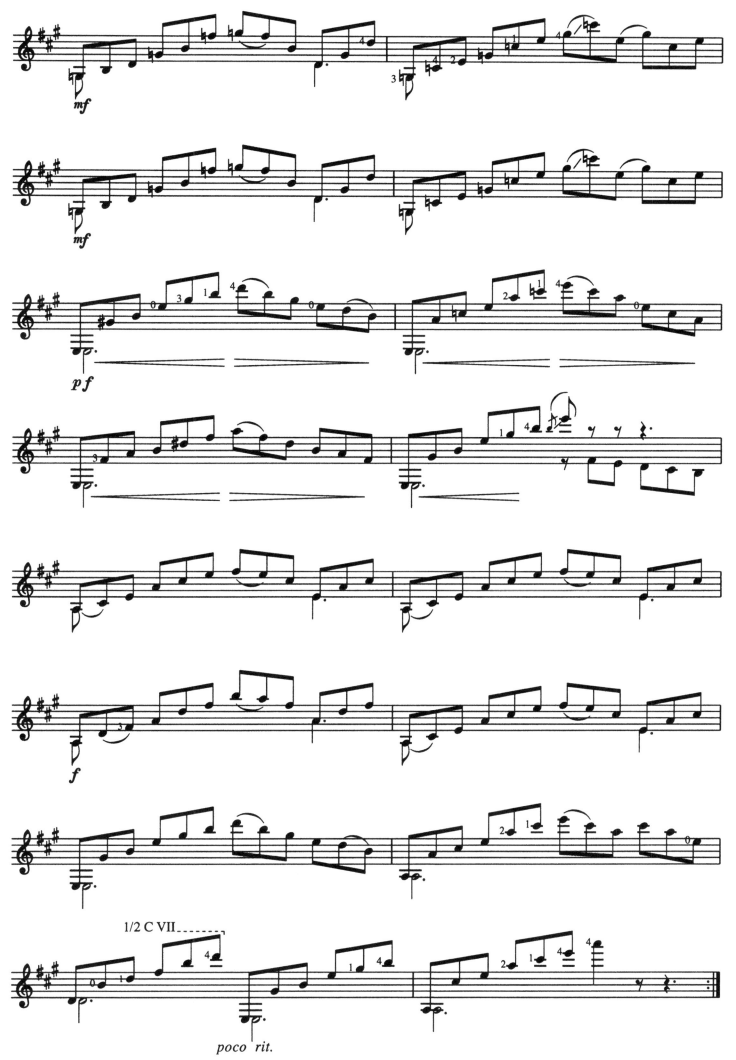

No. 21

D.C. al Fine

No. 22

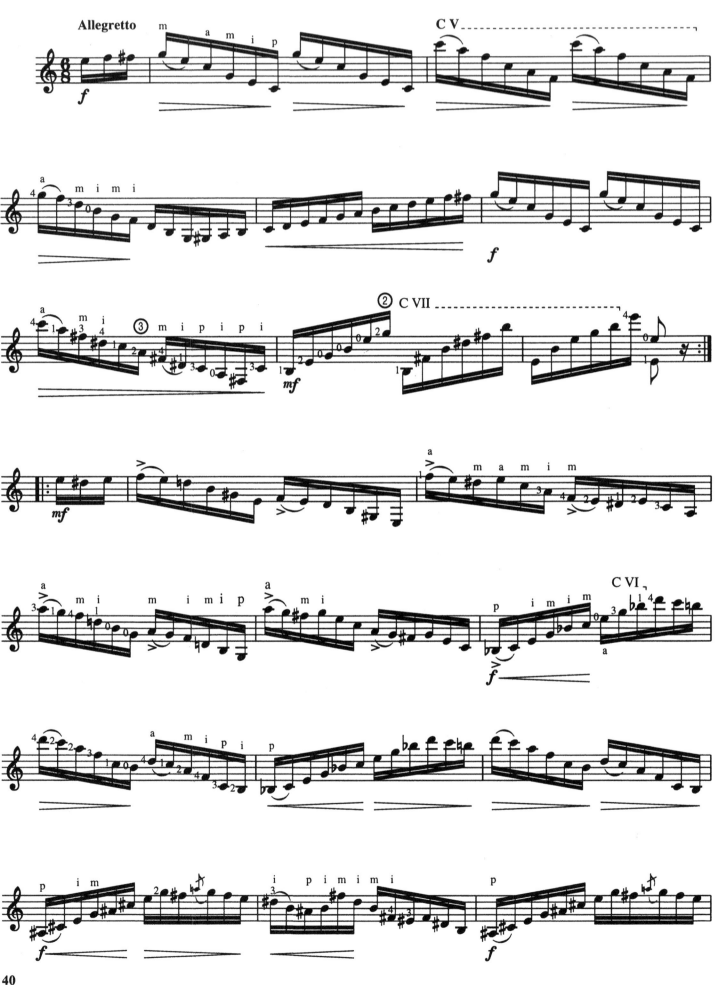

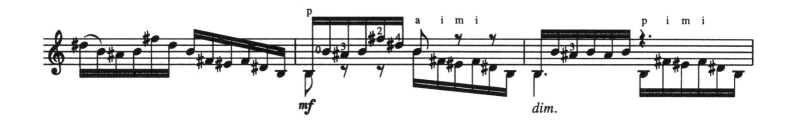

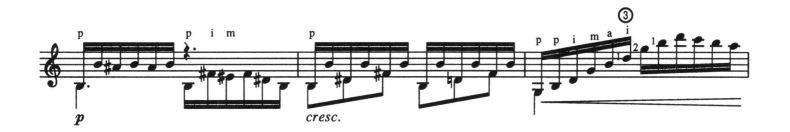

No. 23

No. 24

No. 25

Allegro brillante

CLASSICAL GUITAR

INSTRUCTIONAL BOOKS & METHODS AVAILABLE FROM HAL LEONARD

CLASSICAL STUDIES FOR PICK-STYLE GUITAR
by William Leavitt
Berklee Press

This Berklee Workshop, featuring over 20 solos and duets by Bach, Carcassi, Paganini, Sor and other renowned composers, is designed to acquaint intermediate to advanced pick-style guitarists with some of the excellent classical music that is adaptable to pick-style guitar. With study and practice, this workshop will increase a player's knowledge and proficiency on this formidable instrument.

50449440...$14.99

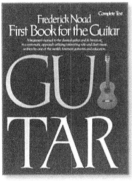

ÉTUDES SIMPLES FOR GUITAR
by Leo Brouwer
Editions Max Eschig

This new, completely revised and updated edition includes critical commentary and performance notes. Each study is accompanied by an introduction that illustrates its principal musical features and technical objectives, complete with suggestions and preparatory exercises.

50565810 Book/CD Pack.......................................$26.99

FIRST BOOK FOR THE GUITAR
by Frederick Noad
G. Schirmer, Inc.

A beginner's manual to the classical guitar. Uses a systematic approach using the interesting solo and duet music written by Noad, one of the world's foremost guitar educators. No musical knowledge is necessary. Student can progress by simple stages. Many of the exercises are designed for a teacher to play with the students. Will increase student's enthusiasm, therefore increasing the desire to take lessons.

50334370 Part 1...$12.99
50334520 Part 2...$18.99
50335160 Part 3...$16.99
50336760 Complete Edition...................................$32.99

HAL LEONARD CLASSICAL GUITAR METHOD
by Paul Henry

This comprehensive and easy-to-use beginner's guide uses the music of the master composers to teach you the basics of the classical style and technique. Includes pieces by Beethoven, Bach, Mozart, Schumann, Giuliani, Carcassi, Bathioli, Aguado, Tarrega, Purcell, and more. Includes all the basics plus info on PIMA technique, two- and three-part music, time signatures, key signatures, articulation, free stroke, rest stroke, composers, and much more.

00697376 Book/Online Audio (no tab) $16.99
00142652 Book/Online Audio (with tab) $17.99

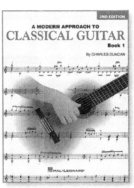

A MODERN APPROACH TO CLASSICAL GUITAR
by Charles Duncan

This multi-volume method was developed to allow students to study the art of classical guitar within a new, more contemporary framework. For private, class or self-instruction.

00695114 Book 1 – Book Only................................$8.99
00695113 Book 1 – Book/Online Audio................$12.99
00699204 Book 1 – Repertoire Book Only............$11.99
00699205 Book 1 – Repertoire Book/Online Audio .$16.99
00695116 Book 2 – Book Only................................$8.99
00695115 Book 2 – Book/Online Audio................$12.99
00699208 Book 2 – Repertoire.............................$12.99
00699202 Book 3 – Book Only................................$9.99
00695117 Book 3 – Book/Online Audio................$14.99
00695119 Composite Book/CD Pack....................$32.99

100 GRADED CLASSICAL GUITAR STUDIES
Selected and Graded by Frederick Noad

Frederick Noad has selected 100 studies from the works of three outstanding composers of the classical period: Sor, Giuliani, and Carcassi. All these studies are invaluable for developing both right hand and left hand skills. Students and teachers will find this book invaluable for making technical progress. In addition, they will build a repertoire of some of the most melodious music ever written for the guitar.

14023154...$29.99

CHRISTOPHER PARKENING GUITAR METHOD
THE ART & TECHNIQUE OF THE CLASSICAL GUITAR

Guitarists will learn basic classical technique by playing over 50 beautiful classical pieces, 26 exercises and 14 duets, and through numerous photos and illustrations. The method covers: rudiments of classical technique, note reading and music theory, selection and care of guitars, strategies for effective practicing, and much more!

00696023 Book 1/Online Audio $22.99
00695228 Book 1 (No Audio) $17.99
00696024 Book 2/Online Audio $22.99
00695229 Book 2 (No Audio) $17.99

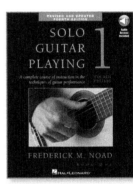

SOLO GUITAR PLAYING
by Frederick M. Noad

Solo Guitar Playing can teach even the person with no previous musical training how to progress from simple single-line melodies to mastery of the guitar as a solo instrument. Fully illustrated with diagrams, photographs, and over 200 musical exercises and repertoire selections, these books offer instruction in every phase of classical guitar playing.

14023147 Book 1/Online Audio $34.99
14023153 Book 1 (Book Only) $24.99
14023151 Book 2 (Book Only) $19.99

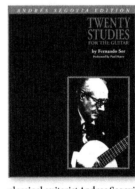

TWENTY STUDIES FOR THE GUITAR
ANDRÉS SEGOVIA EDITION
by Fernando Sor
Performed by Paul Henry

20 studies for the classical guitar written by Beethoven's contemporary, Fernando Sor, revised, edited and fingered by the great classical guitarist Andres Segovia. These essential repertoire pieces continue to be used by teachers and students to build solid classical technique. Features 50-minute demonstration audio.

00695012 Book/Online Audio $22.99
00006363 Book Only..$9.99